A Kept Promise

Debra Ann Barré

DIVACITY PRESS

Copyright © 2006 by Debra Ann Barré. All rights reserved. No part of this work may be reproduced, stored or transmitted in any form or by any means without prior written consent of Debra Ann Barré and/or Divacity Press.

Opinions expressed in this book are those of the author and are offered as general guidelines for success. A certain degree of common sense and an understanding of one's own situation should be considered when applying the advice in this book (or advice in any form).

Cover design by Lee Clevenger and R. Preston Ward
Back cover photo of Miss Barré by Tom Griggs

ISBN Number 0-9764052-8-8
First printing, June 2006.

Published by:

DIVACITY PRESS, a division of:

ThomasMax Publishing
P O Box 250054
Atlanta, GA 30325
www.thomasmax.com

For my Mother and Father, Dolly and Ronald, who have been a constant inspiration my whole life. There are not enough words to express my gratitude for your care and the faith you instilled in me. Thank you for all the love. I have been blessed by God to have you in my life.

TABLE OF CONTENTS

THOUGHTS, POEMS AND VERSES..................4

ACT AS IF IT WERE..11

LIFE! LIVE IT FULLY EVERDAY......................17

NO VALIDATION NEEDED...............................26

POSITIVITY IS A NECESSITY..........................33

TESTED FAITH...43

GO FOR IT...,....54

DRIVEN BY WAY OF GOD...............................67

WHAT GOES AROUND COMES AROUND.........72

CARRY ON...76

UNDER CONSTRUCTION................................82

BE GOOD TO YOURSELF................................88

GET OVER IT!..92

A word from the author

A very special thank you to everyone that has touched my heart and soul. It would take an entire book to thank you all.

First and foremost: my Almighty God. Without you, there's no reason to continue.

Mom and Dad, you have gone far beyond your call of duty.

My brothers and sister who have been the best support team . . . Tony, Ronnie, Donald, Ron-Ron and Keisha, much love.

All my nieces and nephews, you keep me young and laughing.

All my aunts and uncles, you've spoiled me rotten.

I have the best cousins in the world.

Roy Ayers, Jr. We go a long way back.

Robert Ward. I wish the world could have a friend like you.

Ray Hands. Thanks for the inspiration you never knew you gave.

Swayne Family. You kept me on my P's and Q's.

Racuia West. Thanks for the extra push.

Marcy Lewis. Girl, we can burn up the phone lines.

Anna Maria. You made Rome a home.
Cory Nahoum. Who could ever forget you?
Shelton Baily. I finally can clap my hands.
All the cool people I met on my travels.
Shawn and Nooney. Hey there.
Mesha, Celia, Ruthie and Lamar, who helped

me along the way.

Thanks to Lee and Preston at ThomasMax Publishing.

If there is anyone or anything I left out in error, please forgive me.

Thanks everyone for all the love!!!!! Stop! Stop! More! More!

THOUGHTS, POEMS AND VERSES

THOUGHTS FOR THE DAYS

Diamonds are not to be treated like glass.
Humanity is a graceful experience.
Inhale your desires, exhale the drama.
You have the key to unlock the chains on you.
You are as good as you think you are.
You can not expect someone to love or believe in you. . . if you don't love or believe in yourself.
Negative people see the problem. Positive people see the solution.
Only you determine your state of mind.
Winning isn't about the chances you are given. It's about the chances you take.
There are no mistakes—only lessons.
Every dark day has two light ones ahead.
No good deed is ever done in vain.
Don't let the complexities of life deflate your balloon.
Be bold by choice.
Who says you can't have it all?
Your dreams must be bigger than your fears.
Over the top and out of the box is the direction I am heading.

Best way to solve a problem is to avoid it.

Add life to your years, not years to your life.

You are infinitely precious. Nothing and no one can alter that.

Significant times spent with self are priceless.

Today is the last day I will live beneath my desires.

Be electrified by being who you are.

Capitalize on your gifts.

I'm going to put my head on my shoulders, yet!

Success isn't measured by one's accomplishments, but by the obstacles one overcomes.

Focusing on other's abilities is self defeating. Attend to your own.

You will not be invited to the celebration if you don't know where it is.

I believe I'm right where God wants me to be.

Who ever thought there'd be a price to pay for being kind.

What we radiate, we attract.

Lead by example.

If you lose in the first half, go back in the third quarter and up your game.

Become what you inspire others to become.

Make life an adventure to remember.

In physics it is a proven fact for every action there is a reaction.

You will arrive to your destiny if you continue placing one foot in front of the other.

You are in charge of your thoughts, actions and attitudes.

It's nice to be important, but it's important to

be nice.
> God's favorite people are not always favored.
> I'm taking myself off the waiting list.
> Opinions never pay the bills.
> Negative energy creates misery.
> Lord, can I please have patience. Now!
> Bounce back after failure.
> If you reach the limit, then raise the bar.
> Create strategies and overcome all obstacles.

Poems and My point of view

Looking from within
This time I must win
Giving life my best
Who has time for regrets?
Finger pointing gets you nowhere
The nonsense I can no longer bear
Stepping up to the plate
What time is there to hesitate?
*****

Today is all I know
I will relax and let it flow
God, Please show me which
Way to go
Help me to give my all
On you, I will continue to call
*****

Dark days will go away
Don't deviate or go astray
I promise you
It'll be okay
The road is trying
There's no denying

A Kept Promise

Keep your lion's heart
And continue to do your part
You will win
If you don't give up
Or give in

*****

So many emotions
So many things to do
Thoughts of the process of the things
That needs to get done
Can be overwhelming

*****

Overcoming obstacles—
There's no avoiding them
Nor escaping them
They stop by to challenge
Our desires, interrupting our daily routine
They cause some people not to persist any farther
I'm convinced they have their purpose
The purpose, in my opinion, is to see how willing
We are to go after what we want

*****

Fighting for sanity
Searching for peace
Struggling with demons
Let me out!
Stop! No more!
Today I start
Looking from within
Deep within
It's time to take total control of
Who I am
Who I want to be
It's time to let go

Of all ties
That holds me down
It's time to touch
My deepest feelings
Get to know them
And do something about it
Who am I really?
What am I trying to do?
It's time
To find out.

*****

Satisfying your soul's desire should be what you depend on to take you higher.

*****

After you have done all that is required, let the universe do the rest.

*****

Each man is the architect of his own dreams and desires.

*****

Like a soldier
I will continue
To stand
If life pushes too hard
On my feet
I will always land
Temporary set-backs
Are not a fact
My heart sings a strong song
And I will sing it out loud
All the way home

*****

Listening to His voice
He lets us know

That we have a choice
To follow Him
And have no regrets
Or continue to live life in fret

*****

Everyday I'm reaching
For the sky
Every night I pray
That tomorrow
Will turn out right
Constantly trying to unclog
My inner dialogue
Never willing nor ready
To quit
When life gets tough
I get a tighter grip
I may slip
But never fall
I know it will come together
After all

Favorite Bible Verses

"Let us hold fast the confession of our hope without wavering for he who promised is faithful." Hebrews 10:23

"Therefore he promised with an oath to give her whatever she may ask for." Matthew 14:7

"Remember the word to your servant upon you have caused me to hope." Psalms 119:49

"A happy heart makes the face cheerful." Proverbs 15:13

"If you can?" said Jesus. "Everything is possible for him who believes." Mark 9:23

"If the Lord had not been on our side." Psalms 124:1

"Surely he will save you from the fowler's snare and from the deadly pestilence." Psalms 91:3

Favorite Quote

"Things may come to those who wait, but only things left behind by those who hustle." Abraham Lincoln

A Kept Promise is a book about positive uplifting motivational inspirational sayings, quotes and poems.

When I was lying in the intensive care unit with tubes everywhere, I was praying to God with such intensity that my next breath would not be my last. The doctors were not issuing any forms of hope due to a failing heart condition. As I muscled enough energy to turn my head towards the ticking clock on the wall, I saw it was ten before midnight and the only thought I could entertain was to live life. God, if you allow me to live, if you get me out of this bed, I will go beyond any expectation. I will live life with a vivacious, spontaneous, grateful, alive spirit and will inspire many along the way. If I can do that, then my promise has been kept.

We all have what it takes. The true gift is realizing it.

ACT AS IF IT WERE

  I am such a believer in the impossible. Faith is a very special tool. It is like a parachute useless if not used. Of course, everything is wonderful when life is great. But can you keep that smile on your face when every door around you is closed and closed tight? When the windows are locked, can you stand up and truly honestly say without a doubt that everything will be alright and mean it! When the storm is raging and the clouds are dark , do you know in your heart that you will find a way out?

  Act as if it were. Know that without a shadow of a doubt it will work out. Know that the drama is just a test (beep). Know that this is so temporary. Always see the outcome. Never focus on distractions. Stop looking at what you can't do, and focus on what you can. If you want something bad enough, claim it and head toward it. Don't settle for the valley, if the mountain is your aim. It is so easy to lose focus. The moment things become difficult or challenging, it's easy to put things on hold. You must keep your goals and your dreams lit. Whatever it is you're going through, know that things will turn out for good. There's no need to stress your body out for any unnecessary reason. It will work out. It always does, doesn't it?   Sit down and see everything. How you want it to turn out. Plant your seeds. Water the seeds. Mark my words, "step by step, it will all come to pass."

  I remember for my 21st birthday I wanted to

go to Paris. Paris, France, that is! There was this small little problem. I didn't have any cash. I had a job and bills, and my 21st birthday wasn't too far away. All I knew was I was going to be in Paris. Keep in mind I had negative two dollars in my bank account. I saw myself on that plane. I saw myself at the Eiffel Tower. My heart saw it. There it was claimed!

Before long, things fell right into place. The hotel at which I was working was connected to the Hilton. I was able to get a free room for five days and fifty percent off of the food. My friend saw that I was serious and joined me and offered to pay for the food since the room was free. I found the cheapest flight. There I was celebrating my twenty first birthday in Miss Paris France. Despite being overdrawn at the bank by two dollars. Despite people laughing at me and thinking I was crazy when I told them I was going. I saw it. I claimed it. I will never forget that year. Breakfast in Paris. Lunch in New York. Dinner in Los Angeles. Sounds grand! Truth of the matter is, on the way from Paris on the plane, I had a croissant. The hour delay in New York City was a hot dog at the airport and dinner in Los Angeles was with my family. Claim it. See it as if it were, despite the situation.

While writing this book, one of the things I did was to visualize it on the shelves. I saw myself handing them out, even the days when my mind drew a big blank. I was so many pages behind. I acted as if it were. And as you can see, it came to pass. Thank you God!! If the storm has hit you hard and all your luck seems to have run out, don't give up. Know that this too will pass and see it the way you want it to turn out. Miracles only happen to those who believe in them. You will not receive anything if you're not expecting. If you have gained weight and it's taken you forever and a day to lose half a pound, it's ok. Go ahead and visualize the body you want, then work on it. Stop complaining about it and do something. Enough already! The power of visualizing is power. What is it that you want to attract your way?

Some people become discouraged when things don't work out fast enough or results have not arrived. Concentrate on the outcome. Focus on the grand finale. Try a different route. Know when to be still. If you ask God to enlarge your territory, know that He will. As your territory is enlarged, ask for strength to deal with the growing pains. As your heart is being renewed, ride with the wave.

I recall when a couple of my friends were moving to Australia. They were facing challenge after challenge. They did not pay attention to the obstacles, only to the outcome! They saw it as if it were. Two years later, they couldn't be happier.
Claim victory in the midst of defeat. Claim winning. Time and time again! Claim your vision and your destination. Claim life as you want it. Claim your peace of mind. Claim all the good that can possibly come your way.

Claim success.

Claim only the best. You are worth it.

Tame your mind! Positive thoughts only.

When you keep an open mind, it's easier to flow with the twists and turns along life's path.

From the woman who became single after years and years of marriage, to the person sitting behind bars, to the business owner who just lost his business or struggling to keep it, to the one that can not leave drugs alone—take a moment. This very instant. Stop what you are doing and close your eyes. Go ahead close them and see your way out of the temporary situation that has come upon you. See it from beginning to end. With a fierce vision and hard work, life has no choice but to go your way. Your lifestyle determines how you see yourself.

Formulate your plan in your mind. Stamp it, seal it, and I guarantee you it will be delivered. Know it! Know it! Know it! It has to work out. Do not make room for doubt. "Maybe" is a word that should be deleted from your vocabulary. Be careful with the thoughts you entertain. What you think about comes about. Use your energy as a magnet towards the things you desire. Like magic, it will come to pass.

Your circumstance may be far out of control. You may be in the lowest part of the pit. Perhaps you are on your last string and that's about to break. Hold on to that vision as if you were on a mechanical bull (do you know how fast they can go?). Sometimes, your vision is all you have.

It does not matter what has been taken from you or what you've lost. It's all right. You can't cry about it forever. Okay, for a second or two. Keep in mind life carries on!

Everything that I truly, deeply yearned for, I claimed. Far in advance. When that spark lights up within me, there's no stopping. Once the fire gets started, it's a done deal. When your mind takes a mental photo of your desires, you will see how things come to pass just as you pictured it. If you don't see it, how can you expect anyone else to? If you don't believe in you, no one else will! People follow people who are going somewhere. If you're not sure which way you're heading, act as if you know. No one has to know your life is under construction. Present yourself as the finished product. Peek into the future for the outcome you want and feel that moment. Smell it . . . inhale it . . . taste it. Nourish those thoughts on a regular basis. Let the truth be told. Your dreams will surely unfold.

Please! Do not let people talk you out of your visions. If you allow it, some will have you doubting yourself. If you are the only one who believes it, so be it. Impossible is nothing!
Thank God in advance for your miracle. Know that he's just waiting for the perfect time to bring you into your own. I know it may sound impossible right now. Claim the reward before the war is over. Never stay focused on your losses. Update your visions and live them.

God knows all your wants and your needs. He has each and every one of your desires on his "to do" list. Act as if it were. Truth is, He's already taken care of it. If you're worrying about it, then you have doubt. Doubt, my friend, will lead downhill.

The funny thing about planning the trip to Paris was at the time it all seemed impossible. The more obstacles I came across, the stronger my desires became. I was not going to have it any other way. It did not matter to me that my savings were below zero and my bills were about high. Let me tell you, believing is a very important powerful force.

LIFE! LIVE IT FULLY EVERY DAY

Good Morning life
I am happy to see you . . .
Be patient with me
Until I figure out what to do
This soul of mine
Wants to come out and shine
Spend enough days
Settling
It's time for the next phase
Grabbing life by the horns
It's necessary this dream of mine
Is born
Learned from the mistakes of
The past
It's time to enjoy
It's going by so fast

*****

The moment you open your eyes, the rest is fringe benefits. The gift of life is awesome. It's not to be taken lightly. I embrace each day with great enthusiasm. I am so happy to be here. I'm happy that God thought enough of me to breathe life into my existence. Sitting around complaining about what you do not have is a slap in God's face. Be thankful for what you have and work what you have. If you want something that you do not have, you have to go after it. Federal Express is not going to deliver it to your door. I know. I've waited. Just because things are not the way you want them to be does not give you a pass to gripe about them. It will work out.

Keep life fun and exciting. Take time to enjoy the small things in life. Simple things such as opening up your eyes and watching the sun set.
Life is to be embraced. Not just on special occasions or holidays or when you think of something good that has happened to you.

You woke up this morning! That alone should be enough to make you want to do a cartwheel. Your life is like a blank canvas, and *you* are the artist. God is first, without a doubt. Find things that excite you . . . things that keep your adrenaline flowing. Sometimes you have to be your own marching band. If necessary, the entire parade.

If life happens to give you lemons, I suggest you to make lemonade. I travel with a bag of sugar. Remember the day that matters: every day! Everyday is a reason to be delighted with happiness. Everyday is a reason for a smile.

Believe me, I know that sometimes at the beginning it starts out fantastic, la tee de and la tee da!. During the course of the day, people and things slowly start deflating your balloon, and by the end of the day, you feel as if you've been run over by a herd of elephants. Maintain your sanity when this happens. It's easier said than done. I can tell you how to have the most optimistic attitude ever. I'm becoming better at practicing what I preach. It's you that have to keep your own motor running. You

A Kept Promise

must learn to dust off your shoulders all the issues and negative energy from your mind.

Whatever it is that you want, you need to stop thinking about it and get up and move.

You've have the choices and chances. The best time to start is right here and now. Doesn't matter what you've done, where you've been, your age, your background, or your financial status. You have the chance to get it right. If you have it right, work it to keep it.

We all want it all; not many are willing to give what is necessary.

I've always loved putting the extra excitement into life. Years back, I decided I needed a change of scenery. I remember how enchanting Paris was. I loved the European flare. I was living in New York. I decided I wanted to move to Europe. I had a great job, awesome friends, and a very supportive family behind me.

My adventurous streak was taking control. I threw my cares to the wind and flew to California to spend time with my family. Ready, set—ready to go! I chose London for the fact that is was a country where the people spoke English.

The excitement of moving to a whole new country thrilled me so. The thought of a different culture had my adrenaline going 95 m.p.h.! I love being in that euphoric state of mind. There I was on my way to London, England. I did not have one single contact. God has always been on my main line. I knew as long as I had him on my side, I couldn't lose.

I had eighty dollars cash in my pocket . . . and an American Express card . . . and off to London

I went! On the plane I had a couple of strong drinks and passed out. The next thing I knew, the stewardess was waking me up, "Ma'am, Ma'am, you're at Heathrow Airport." Lord. What have I done? As I slowly came to, I realized I was many miles from home. I had actually packed my bags, quit my job and moved to London. (The things I will do for excitement!)

What a blast. It was a new place and a new thrill. I lived there for six months and made the most of it. Then one day, I decided it was time for another new thrill. I wasn't sure if I wanted to go to Rome or to Germany. I could not decide which, so I flipped a coin, and Rome won. Yes! You know it. Off to Rome I went.

There I was, traveling through Italy, not knowing a single soul. My funds were very limited. (This was once again another most impulsive moment.) I totally felt like Dorothy from *The Wizard of Oz*. My first mission was to find some type of work; as long as it was legal, I did not care what it might be. Name it: Nanny, Cook, Translator, Coat check. I wanted to see Rome and, wow, there I was, a long way from home. I was much too excited to be afraid. New friends, new culture and a whole new scene, and I was learning the language. I truly loved it. I ended up staying in Rome for two and a half years. I traveled by train to visit Naples, Venice (loved Venice), Florence and Milan. Wow, just reminiscing thrills me.

There I was, enjoying a vision I had visualized. When I made all my plans to travel to Europe, I did not have a lot of money. I don't suggest going that route! However, my desire was so bloody intense I had to follow my soul. What an experience. I will never forget! Whatever it is you want to do, keep the excitement going. Polish it up a touch. Give life your all, you will never be disappointed.

I completely enjoy each and every day. I have a great passion and deep respect for life. There are so many things to do and so many places to see. What's not to enjoy? I greet each day with a twinkle in my eye. If my insane happiness sickens someone . . . oh well, it sounds like a personal problem. I'm delighted for it all! And tomorrow, I'll feel the same way. I highly suggest *you* open the door to you. Don't shortchange yourself on anything. You deserve it all and then some!

Be willing to try new things. Experience different cultures. Learn a new language. Go ahead, do something out of the ordinary. Make today a bit more interesting than yesterday. Who said the sky had to be the limit? There is no limit to how far you can reach if you dare. Pursue the things that you want. Go after it with all that you have inside of you. If you give little, you will receive little. If you give a lot, you will receive abundance. Take each day to map out your masterpiece. What grace has been put upon us to have this gift of today?

Live life fully every day. Break with the daily routine every once in a while. Change it up! Spice it up! Rearrange it! Life can become boring doing the same thing day after day after day. Live life with great enthusiasm! Live life with a new attitude. The only way to get back excitement is to give it out! Make the best out of every situation. Today will bring about results from your work from yesterday.

If the results are not showing fast enough, work a little harder. Don't get weary. In due time, it will come about.

I decided that I am going to live this life that God has given to me to the absolute fullest . . . to enjoy each and every single second of it. Each day is a parade. If it happens to rain on yours, bring an umbrella.

Today is about learning all you can to be better. When you know better, you do better. Consider how you want to live your life. Choose to be a part of something grand. Life is meant to be an exhilarating experience. Don't worry about tomorrow's lunch when you haven't had your breakfast today. Take a day at a time. Love yourself. You can not be everything to everybody without being something first to yourself. Each day, give yourself the gift of doing something special for you. Your life is a present. Go ahead and put a bow on it.

A good life is a well-lived life. Live your life with meaning. Be that exquisite unique soul that you were created to be. Bring your light to life on a regular basis. Enjoying each day is really easy when you love who you are. You don't have to have someone in your life to make you happy. Being alone doesn't mean loneliness. You create your own happiness. So today, find yourself something to love. A good place to start is with you.

God has made an awesome plan for our lives. Isn't that enough to get some excitement going? Shake it up a bit and find that joy in life. Light that spark that's begging to be lit.

Life is more than just about work. Don't be

so busy trying to make a living that you don't have a life. You can never get this day back. Try to enjoy all that comes your way today, and if it's not the best day, make the most of it. Your personal happiness is your own responsibility. Since it's up to you to enjoy it, then you are the blame if you are not living life to the absolute fullest.

Use all the parts of yourself. Add color to your life. Don't wait for anyone to roll out the red carpet for you. Travel with your own at all times. You are as grand as you believe. If you were to find out that you had a day to live, how would you spend it? What would or wouldn't you do? I'm willing to bet you one thing for sure, you would not spend half of the time on the nonsense that you do. Am I right? So why not let today be a good day? Change your attitude towards life.

You notice when children celebrate their birthdays, they embrace them with such triumph and excitement. One grows older into adulthood, and the fire slowly starts to fizzle out. Some people act ashamed of their ages. Why?? There is no shame in growing older. Just do it gracefully. I am extremely proud to be here alive and well at forty-three. Yes, forty-three and somewhat sane. Okay, I will go ahead and brag a little. When a twenty-two year old asks me out, that does the ego good. Don't let your fire fizzle through the years. I feel better than I did when I was eighteen years old. I may not know all what to do, but I know what not to do. One lesson learned is this gift of life is not to be taken for granted.

Keep life new. Do not allow the days to drift into one another. Each day is new. Treat it as that.

Leave all ugly issues in yesterday. Today does not deserve to pay for yesterday's mistakes. Life is a one-way ticket. This is one way trip whether you are eight or eighty—live it up! Today is a day filled with endless possibilities and great expectations. Why not greet it with open arms?

Having the time of your life is something you should make a full-time effort. Life is as grand as you think it is! Experience!

About two weeks ago, I lost one of my special cousins. What sadness came upon me upon realizing that was my fifth cousin under the age of forty that had spread his wings and flown away much too soon. I feel any that age is too young to exit, but to go so young with so much life that could have been left . . . wow!

Life owes no explanations. It will force you to take absolutely nothing for granted. The things that seem so drastic before becomes so minor.

Life is much too short to live it as a spectator. You code the combination to unlock your safe . . . the safe that holds your true valuables.

Applause is good, but a standing ovation is what your life should be about. I gave mediocrity its walking papers and have no intentions or desires to invite it back.

`Live your life so when you die, you are the one smiling and everyone else is crying.

My strategy is to enjoy each second of this privileged gift of life. I laugh every chance I get and keep a positive attitude no matter what! I will run this race with my head held high. I will welcome all that is good. I'm no longer searching anything or anyone to make me feel special. The clouds are lifted, and I realize I'm gifted. Life is all it's cracked up to be and then some.

Get in the mindset that each day offers the opportunity to make something wonderful happen. Do you not think it's time to give your life some exclamation points?!!!

I am an adrenaline junkie who loves excitement. I splurge on impulsive thoughts and constantly crave new endeavors. I keep all my *oohs* and *aahs* alive! I savor the flavor life has to offer.

*****

Thought for the days:
Don't get bitter, get better.

NO VALIDATION NEEDED

"All beautiful you are, my darling; there is no flaw in you." Song of Songs 4:7

Others' opinions of you is none of your business. I mean, really, does it matter what someone else thinks? The only validation needed is from God, and He gave that to you the day you were born. You are someone whether someone loves you or not. Those who matter don't mind and those who mind don't matter.

It bothers me when people who think that they are less than they are because they are not in a relationship, or someone has treated them wrong. No need to feel like the air has been let out of your balloon. Okay, they did not return the love. Okay, you gave everything you had and then some. You did things that you can not believe you've done. It's all right!

Letting people rent free space in your head and being affected by people's many mood swings is enough to drive an insane man sane. Oh, we can not forget about the people who think that because you don't have what they think you should have, you're not good enough. Validation does not come from where we live or what we drive. It all comes from within. It comes from knowing who you are. The moment you realize who you are and what you want, it really doesn't matter what someone else's opinion is. I mean, really, when did anyone else's thoughts ever pay one single bill? People are always quick to pick out your flaws quicker than your attributes. Some people feel better putting others down. But do they know, when they are pointing a finger, there's three pointing back at them? So keep your shoulders dusted off and a smile on your face.

I am what I am, and what I am doesn't need excuses. If anyone looks down on you, inform them that the only time you look down on a man is when they are lifting him up.

I decided to take control of me and my emotions and my thoughts and my destiny. No longer was I giving someone else the rope and telling them to pull. No longer am I going to allow anyone's authority to enter my world! If you don't stand for something, you will fall for anything.

Another thing I've learned is that trying to please everyone is the biggest NO-NO! Trying to make everyone else happy will leave you completely miserable. Please God first. Then yourself. It's such a better journey that way. You do not need anyone else's approval by any means! You were approved the day or evening you made your entrance into this world. This is your time. Your moment. You'd better enjoy it. This isn't a dress rehearsal, and as my Aunt would say, "It's time to love you. Everything about you." Whatever situation you're in, it doesn't matter how you look. Love yourself as you are, right now. And if you're not taking care of yourself, right now is a good time to start. Right now is the best time to polish up and do something for you. Never search for your happiness in other people or things. It starts within. You can never change the outside without changing the inside.

You are precious and priceless. You are a rare jewel. And if you are a butterfly caught in a cocoon, you will have your time to fly.

Someone doesn't have to be in your life to validate you. Of course, it's great when that someone special is there. Someone that lights your world. If it's not happening, honey, you have to light your own world.

Express yourself. Love being you. Be your own best friend. Don't worry about fitting in. Lead and never follow. You don't have to wait until someone gives their approval or permission for you to feel approved. Welcome that thing that makes you! You! If you are wearing red while everyone else has on beige, please, wear it well.

Think highly of yourself. There is nothing wrong with tooting your own horn. Being confident is not a sin. It only turns ugly when you lose your humility and begin thinking you are above everyone else—not good. We are all God's children. We have weaknesses and strengths in different areas. We all have our own road to travel. Travel your road with a nonjudgmental attitude. Travel your road welcoming the different qualities in everyone.

Give to people what you want them to give back to you. Stand tall and avoid drama at all costs. Don't compromise your standards for anyone's acceptance.

I used to have this obsessive need to always want to please. Somehow I thought it was my duty. "Please, please help me Lord", I said. Trying to please all, you please none. I learned quickly that the pleasing business wasn't for me. It doesn't matter if it's your spouse, your children, lover, brother, who ever it is, you can't please everyone. The more you do for people, the more they expect you to do. Do not let your world be run according to people and their demands on you. Others' thoughts are just that: others' thoughts. If it's not productive or constructive criticism, do not welcome it. Do not keep company with anyone who can not respect you. They don't have to like you, but they will have to respect you. And please, by all means, start pleasing yourself first. Care about what you think about yourself. That's what really matters.

What sickens me to the core is racism. What a completely uncalled for waste of . . . I don't know what to call it! It is senseless to go around hating someone for the color of his skin. I mean, come on, how pathetic—utilizing all that energy in hate. Only a fool could believe he is better because his ethnicity is different! Give me a break. Please! Let's get rid of all the stereotyping, the labeling, the judging, and by all means, the uncalled-for hate!

One other thing that rubs me the wrong way is when someone becomes jealous due to someone else's success. You must be as happy for the success of others as you are of your own! Why become envious because someone else had the guts to go for his dream? It's enough for everyone. Let's love each other a little more, and I promise some of the issues will disappear. Live your life and let others live theirs. Concentrate on you.

Know you!
Know who you are!
Own it!

Regardless of any flaw, don't allow anyone to make you feel less than you are.

Compare yourself to no one but yourself. You are not under contract to live up to anyone's standards but yours and God's.

Go where you are celebrated and not just tolerated has to be one of my favorite sayings. It says so much. The first person that should celebrate you, of course, is you. Avoid surrounding yourself with people who tolerate you. You are a diamond. Don't allow someone to treat you like glass.

You're the keeper of your soul. You and only you own the key. Stop making copies and giving them away.

You have been given the right to be yourself. There's no need to explain you to anyone. Next time someone tries to tell you of your shortcomings, give them a mirror and then say, "First you look . . . ."

We all have our beliefs, our own opinions, and our own ways life! Period! One way isn't better than the other. Why do we always want people to convert or revert to our lifestyle . . . our way of doing things? Let it be! The best gift you can give yourself and others is the right to be free. Free your spirit. I'm learning on a daily basis to love me and accept myself. I can not expect someone else to accept me if I don't accept myself. I'm learning to love it all: the shortcomings and flaws. I'm okay, even if in my own mind.

I could knock myself on the head when I think of a few past situations where I felt less of myself due to someone's thoughts of me. Once again, "If I knew then what I know now." Never again! Now I know my worth and it's priceless!

Each of us has an area that can use a little work. Who needs assistance when their shortcomings are being magnified? I know I don't.

I'm tired of people who have egos larger than football fields. Come on, Earth to ego trippers! Validation has nothing at all to do with your status. It's about your heart.

We all want to be heard, to fit in and to belong. No one wants to be excluded. You are only excluded if you consent to it. Looking for acceptance outside ourselves is not a direction anyone should travel.

Refuse to reduce who you are for anyone if someone doesn't like you. Do not take it personally. Nothing at all is wrong with you. Let's face it, some people's chemistries just do not mix. Acceptance should not be a daily battle. Find comfort with who you are.

*****

Thought for the day:
No one can make you feel bad about yourself without your consent.

POSITIVITY IS A NECESSITY

Optimistic (adjective): A positive attitude; cheerful, hopeful, buoyant, confident.

With words like these, how can one lose?

Staying positive is a total must. Yes, it is easier said than done. Positive attitude brings upon positive situations. Always focus on the solution and not the problem. What the devil meant as messing, God will turn around as a blessing. Know that your current situation does not decide your future outcome. Things may look a total disaster and you may feel like throwing in the towel, but that's when you need to recharge your battery and take a deep breath. Count to ten, maybe to twenty, and get up and try again. Never make quitting an option. No guts—no glory. The story doesn't change.

Positive thoughts are like magnets. You draw to you what your thoughts are. If you think that you will never make it and things are never going to go your way, well—guess what—that is exactly what will happen. But if you think, *yes, it's a bit uncomfortable. However, this is such a temporary situation. Things can only get better from here.* Expect a change, expect it to work out. Know that this is just a matter of time. Tough times don't last. Tough people do.

I, myself, love happy people. Happy people are nice to be around. It feels like a ton of bricks when negative energy is around. It cannot be hidden. Positive people focus on everything that's going right or soon will be going right. Focus on what you have and not on what you don't have.

Staying positive is good for the soul. It keeps you young at heart. I know every day it's a bit of a challenge to always be on top of the world. But if you constantly remind yourself of all the good things, I guarantee you it's easier. One second things are going totally according to plan, then all of a sudden you feel like you need an elevator just to get to the curb. Those are the times when you need to hold your head up high and continue to continue. Trust me when I tell you positivity is a necessity. Attitudes are contagious. Is yours worth catching?

Some people are unhappy and do not like to see it when you're always in a good mood. They're having a bad day, and they want company. Life is much to short to spend any of it in misery. Through all the drama and all the nonsense, always manage to keep a great outlook on life. I say why feel good when you can feel great? I look at my glass as half full and not half empty. If you ever get fired from a job, don't look at it as if you lost the job . . . the job lost you. Positive Mental Attitude (PMA) is a must.

Make the most of right now. Keep a smile on your face in the midst of adversity. Let go of the entire negative luggage. Let go of all negative thoughts. Do not replay in your mind all of your mistakes. Learn from them.

Encourage yourself! Rise above things that will bring you down. Keep doing the right thing even when the wrong thing is done to you. Don't wait for something great to happen to you before you get optimistic and have a positive attitude. Get happy now. Find something that makes you feel good and make it happen!

I've always have kept a positive outlook on life. I refuse to allow what's wrong outweigh what's right. You should always count your blessings. I'm intoxicated with enthusiasm.

I thought when I got married that my Prince Charming had ridden right in out of the night. I thought I had struck gold. I was looking for someone else to supply my happiness. I depended on him to make me feel complete. I thought my world had ended when the marriage failed. I could not believe how distraught I was. I dried my tears and realized I still had God and I have myself.

I know now God moves what isn't right for us out of the way to make room for what is.

Everything we look for is within us. God has given us all the pieces of the puzzle. It's up to us to put them together. I made my mind up that I will stay up and happy. I'm an optimistic fool. My energy is overflowing. I know without a doubt of doubts that God is working it out for me. He already has. He's my father. I'm his child. Case closed!

Positive energy keeps you young and well. It's not what happens to you in life; it's your attitude towards it.

A true positive attitude is when things are not going your way and the sun is nowhere in sight and you're able to smile as if you won the lottery. If you feel good on the inside, it shows. If you feel great, it will attract great things to you. Whatever we think is what will come our way.

Positivity is a necessity by all means!

Please folks do not let anyone at any time steal your joy. If you want to be happy, go ahead. You have that right. You own your attitude. You have control of your emotions.

Stay away from people with pins ready to pop your bubble. People will pick you apart from head to toe if you let them. They will rip you to shreds. No one deserves that kind of power over you! Do you not agree?

Some people do not understand my nonstop, over the top, ninety-nine point nine percent of the time being a complete hopeless optimist. They say, "What is she on? No one can be that damn happy at all times." Truth of the matter: I am totally delighted to have awakened this morning. I'm so busy counting my blessings that there's no time to concentrate on anything else. I'm here another day. I have another chance to get it right.

Bad vibes and negative energy are no longer allowed within my surroundings. I've chosen not to acknowledge in any form whatsoever of wickedness. None! Positive plus positive equals positive. If you're doing everything in your power and your attitude is nonstop up and optimistic, you can not help but win. Win! Win!

If you can stay sane, it'll work out. I am not accepting anything less than.

Positivity is a necessity. Not every once in a while, but each and everyday. It's a must to give out what you want back. I want a good happy carefree completely drama free and stress free journey.

A Kept Promise

Just like the dream catcher that catches the good and filters out the bad, avoid inhaling negative energy, as it is toxic to the soul. Don't allow people to bring you down to their level of mess. Life can be challenging, dealing with your own issues. Who needs assistance with more crap? I don't. I've learned that I cannot save the world. It's a full time job trying to save myself. Work on what makes you feel good about you.

Eating right and working out contributes to feeling great. Working out definitely relaxes the nervous system. You don't have to be a health fanatic or gym buff. But at least make an effort to move towards a healthier life style. You are never too young or old to start being healthy. Certain foods have something to do with your mood swings. Think about it. If you're constantly gulping down heavy greasy food, it will have an effect on how you're feeling. Be sure to drink lots of water. Think of yourself as a plant. A plant becomes dull and dried when not watered.

Keep your organs happy. Fresh fruit and vegetables do wonders to the body. Take care of the only body you've been given.

Daily I ask God for strength. Daily I recharge my batteries. Sometimes hourly. The more I tell myself that no one is going to get my energy . . . *Boom!* Out of nowhere comes a test, and sometimes it's a funky test. It's that ugly energy from someone trying to work your spare nerve. People can only change your mood if you let them. It's totally up to you if you're going to give someone that kind of authority over you. Shame on you if you do! I totally admit that was me once upon a time walking around feeling like I'm on top of the world tiptoeing through the tulips, all was completely grand. Then chaos comes knocking at my door totally uninvited. Trying to see how long it's going to take before I lose all sense of sensibility. Well, off the edge I went. What a waste of precious time to ever have allowed someone's negative attitude to change my state of mind. I've learned to put my shoulders back, my stomach in, and keep stepping. I'm a very happy, nonstop, energized, motivated, positive fun loving high-spirited person. I enjoy this precious life with my entire being. Positive thoughts bring about positive things.

I have chosen to go where I'm celebrated and not tolerated. And this light of mine, I will let it shine. God gave it to me and the world would not take it away. I believe whatever it is that you believe, you will receive. Through it all, hold on to your sanity. Once you truly have you, and other people are not running your emotions, you're good to go.

Are you an optimist or a pessimist? Are you always looking at the best of a situation or the worst in a situation?

It is true; life is ten percent of what happens to you and ninety percent of how you handle it. If something happened to you ten years ago and you are still bitter about it, you need to take some time and do some cleaning. As often as possible, you need to clean out all the bitterness and anger. These are things that can hinder your spirit. Inhale the good, exhale the bad. Just as you would do spring cleaning to your home, you need to do spiritual cleaning to your soul.

A great personality will take you a long way. People like to be around people who make them feel good. Make yourself worthwhile being around. Do not carry your worries on your sleeve. Why carry what someone did or didn't do twenty or thirty years ago? Free your mind from all garbage. Smile at the world and the world will smile back. Optimistic people live better and longer lives.

Let's talk about keeping a sense of humor. About seven years ago, I was on my way from work to visit my sister and nephews with two weeks of pay in my pocket, ready to enjoy the weekend. It was drizzling a bit as I crossed the street when out of nowhere this Toyota comes and literally knocks my out of my shoes. The impact knocked the stone out of my ring as well as this cute wig I had on. The wig had a French Roll in the back. I picked up my hair and put it back on my head. Yes I did! By this time the French Roll was in the front. I had blood dripping down my face. I was in total shock from what just happened. I could not believe not one single person stopped to help. Wait a minute, one woman did slow down, rolled her window down and attempted to ask if I was okay. Mind you, I just got the wind knocked out of me by a car that hit me and kept going. I wiped the blood that was dripping from a wide gash above my left eye. I told her, "Oh yeah, I'm fine!" She looked amazed and kept on. I managed to walk for five minutes to my sister's. I arrived at the door. Well, you can imagine her expression when opening the door. I was rushed to the hospital. The doctors could not believe that I walked after being hit so hard. I managed to smile through all the fractured bones and my neck brace. My body was aching from head to toe. I laugh now when I think about grabbing my hair before seeking help. Keep your humor through it all.

Focus on the good in everything. Laughter is one life's best medicines. Find a person to laugh with as much as possible or laugh alone as laughter releases endorphins.

You deserve to be happy. Spread your wings and fly. This is your journey. Live for you. Unlock the chains you have allowed others and yourself to put on you. You are not here forever. Enjoy your life, please. One day you are going to have to give up your visitor's pass and check out of here. I highly suggest you make the very best of it.

I can not emphasize how vitally important it is to have a positive attitude. Every once in a while, a bad day will creep in. There are these days when you will go to the edge and sometimes jump. Bounce back. It's all in the attitude. Attitude is everything!

Bad and evil thoughts poison the mind and spirit. Eventually they take their toll, and before you know it, a bitter soul is born. We are all born into happiness. Well, this is my point of view. Turning the tables of life can affect the way you feel, if you allow it.

God knows, I know how challenging it can become when you are trying to maintain sanity. Just when you thought you were on smooth street, bump, there's life keeping you on your toes. Let nothing get you down.

When you are smiling on the inside and you feel good about yourself, people feel it and feed off it. Your attitude determines your altitude.

There's a lot of adulation that comes along with a positive attitude. For starters, you're a pleasure to be around. The weight of the world does not weigh you down. The list goes on . . . . Being that life isn't here forever, why wouldn't you want to enjoy it with a bit more enthusiasm? Your attitude will definitely make or break your spirit. Emotions have a way of controlling our attitude. Put a lid on all of your uncontrolled emotions.

You can not expect happiness to speed-dial you and tell you it has arrived. You have to make that call. Change your attitude and you will change your life! I promise you that!

The universe is composed of spinning wheels of energy. What kind of energy are your wheels spinning?

You may have to work hard to maintain a high level of motivation and excuse all of your discouraging influences. Staying positive is worth all the effort.

Positive affirmations are the antidotes if you want to stay successful.

*****

Thought for the day: Negative people see the problem. Positive people see the solution.

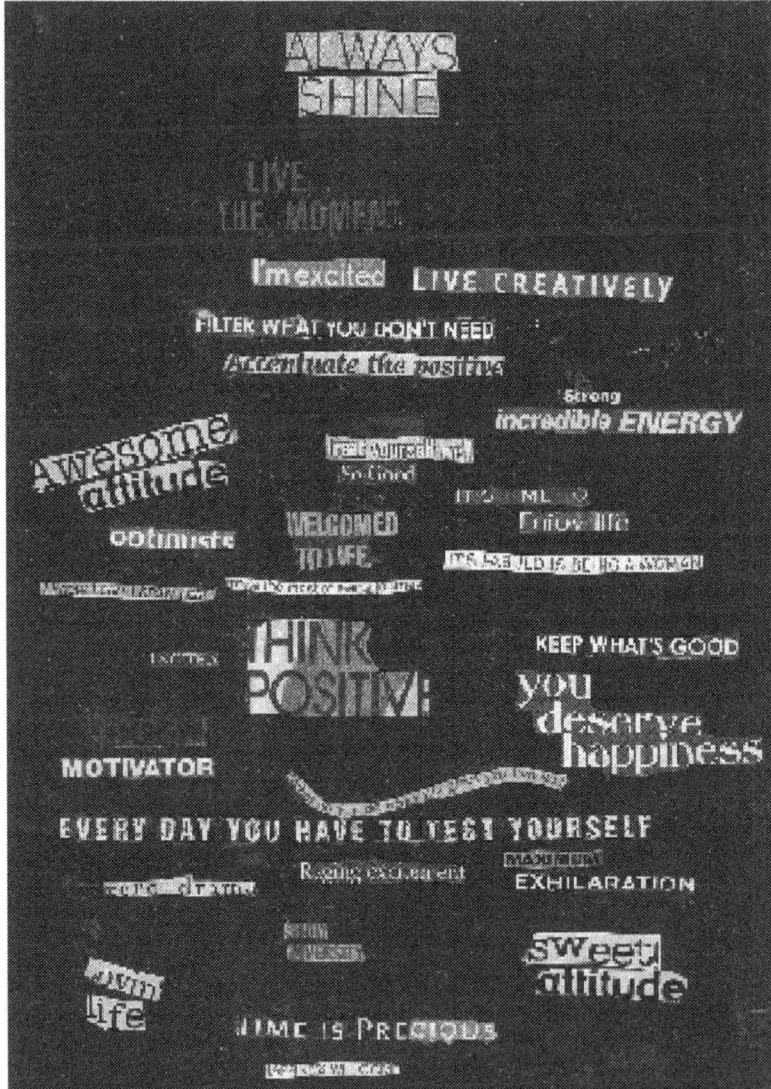

TESTED FAITH

[Handwritten medical progress record from Good Samaritan Hospital, 1225 Wilshire Blvd., Los Angeles, California 90017, dated 3/8/00:]

> To whom it may concern,
>
> Debra Boone has a congenital cardiomyopathy which has progressed to the point where she is now totally disabled with an ejection fraction of only 10. She probably has less than 6 months to live unless she can get a heart transplant. There is no history of drug abuse and her toxicology screens are negative. She becomes very dyspneic with even minimal exertion.
>
> — Dan Schmidt, MD
> 213-977-2121

"My flesh and my heart my fail, but God is the strength of my heart." Psalm 73:26

"For where your treasure is, there your heart will be also." Matthew 6:21

Can I please talk about Tested Faith? Can the Church say "Amen" about Tested Faith?

Faith has brought me through some of my darkest days. Faith has been the light on which I continue to focus. Faith is what kept me sane when I had five cardiologists tell me that if I did not get open-heart surgery that I would die within six months. Each doctor's diagnosis was worse than the previous one's had been. For a second I felt as though I had been run over by a train. If I was looking for hope in those doctors, it would have been over long time ago. I was born with an enlarged heart. Talk about having a big heart! My heart was four times its normal size. Just when I thought all was good to go, my heart decided to give me a run for my faith.

I had to call on my all-mighty Father and pray, "God I know that you did not bring me through all of the dark days to end it here." I decided that I was going to trust Him completely and I do mean completely.

I was like a horse with blinders. All I saw was my complete healing. All I heard was God whispering in my soul: *Child if you trust me, then you need to prove it.* The more I believed that I was being healed, the more times I found myself in the emergency room hooked up to an oxygen machine because I was having breathing difficulties. I repeatedly repeated, "This too shall pass. This is only strengthening my faith." I had to work my faith like a muscle. I grabbed on to my faith so tightly. God stepped in like He always does and said, "Child because you kept the faith, here's your reward." Here it is years later and my heart condition has changed ninety-nine percent . . . for the better, of course! I can outwalk eighteen-year-olds in my high heels, while they have on flats.

Without a doubt, the love of family and true friends helped get me by. By the way, I never had the transplant. I did not care how many doctors said no. My God said and says yes. Faith brought me through that.

Since I was expecting a miracle, I had to do my part. I changed my eating habits and was on one heck of a health ritual. I kept my mind and spirit healthy. When expecting that miracle, play your role in it. Nothing's coming your way if you don't expect or prepare for it. You will run into people saying, "Oh nothing good is going to happen to me. Things will never work out." Etc, etc. And they are right. With an attitude like that, they're stopping their own shows. Act the way you want to live and soon you'll live the way you act.

If you are in a situation that seems gloomy and depressing and the more you try, the more you feel you're running in quicksand, smile anyway. Every time you think you are gliding high on that magic carpet and, *boom*, out of nowhere the carpet is snatched without warning, keep smiling. That you fall down does not mean that you have to stay down. Success is going from failure to failure without the loss of enthusiasm.

As a man thinks, so he is. Be like that tiny cat looking into the mirror and seeing a fierce lion. Your faith will keep you sane in your insane times. Your faith will take you places you have never been before. Your faith will open shut doors. So today I challenge you to go ahead and believe in the impossible. Go ahead; I dare you to take God at His word. He says faith is the substance of things hoped for and the evidence not seen.

How strong is your faith? Does it grow stronger after every trial, or does it weaken with every disappointment? Do not get stuck on pause. (Don't I know that feeling?) Remember the road to a thousand miles begins with one step. The sooner you get moving, the sooner things will go your way. Through the darkest days, buckle up, stand strong and hold on. Hold on like you have never held on before. Your faith is the key that will open up all doors. Faith is what keeps me going. Faith has brought me through every valley depth and mountain top. Faith is such a powerful force. It will cause a mountain to be moved.

God is my all. I turn to Him for everything. I find comfort in His arms. What an awesome feeling knowing He has me covered. All my needs are met. If God is for me, who can be against me? God has kept His promise to me. He told me that He would never leave me nor forsake me. I promised him when I was in ICU that if He gave me just one more chance that I would not take this life for granted. I promised Him to give back to life what life has given me. I promised God that I would make the best out of every situation and conquer every desire within my heart. "Climb every mountain or attempt" is a promise I made to myself as well as to stay committed to something other than insanity. We all go through a test, so we can have a testimony.

One of my favorite gifts given to me by my mom is Faith. If you look in the dictionary for faith, I guarantee my mom's face will be right there. My parents have always made me feel that nothing ever was impossible. If I dared to reach for it, everything was tangible. I'm so glad faith was instilled in my heart from the very beginning. My faith has been tested. I'm glad that I held on and will continue to hold on. When your faith has backbone, you can stand strong. God has your back. That you can count on.

He has been God way before we arrived. He created the mountains and the sea. I know he will take care of me. My faith has been put to the test. Results work out for the best.

I pray all the time, not just when I need something. There's folks who pray for something so diligently, then after it come to pass, their prayers lose intensity. The same enthusiasm you have while asking God for something is the same enthusiasm you should have while thanking Him.

I've seen first-hand after a person has received for what they begged God; they toss it to the side like a day-old newspaper. Okay. I've been guilty of that. After God completely healed me, I went back eating fast foods that clog up my poor arteries. I had to remind myself of the long prayers I had with Him. I promised how I was going to do this and that. How quickly one forgets. It's easy to get off track but you must keep your promise to God or at least attempt to try. When you have faith, giving up is impossible.

I'm following the light that God has instilled within me. I'm not moving from this space of sanity. It's taken too much time to get here. I will trust him with my all. I am not ashamed of who I stand for. I love God! Yes I do. He has confirmed each and every one of my beliefs. He has kept each one of His promises. He has spared my life. I am forever in his debt. Tried! Tested! True!

Don't loose your faith while going through trials and tribulations of life. It's always the darkest before the sun shines the brightest. No doubt about it. Your faith will get tested one way or the other. Bend, if you must, but don't you break. Feel it in the pit of your gut. Breathe it into existence. Don't talk about it. Be about it.

Only the strong survive. It's not where you've been, it's where you're going. It's not how many times you made a mistake; it's how many times you learn from it. If you fall one hundred times, get up one hundred and one times.

Don't get discouraged. You go through a dry season for a reason. Never will God let you evaporate as you fall by the wayside. The truth of the matter is that if you can maintain your sanity through the ups and downs and the twists and turns of life, you're heading towards the right direction.

FAITH: **F**ollow **A**ll **I**nside **T**he **H**eart.

Listen to your heart. Step out on cold faith. Close your eyes and jump knowing that you will have a safe landing.

You cannot be timid. You must stand the test of time. Your faith will continue to be tested. Can you pass? Faith assures you that tomorrow will bring about a brighter day. Faith is the light that lights the soul.

Improve your state of mind. Don't be so quick to jump off the handle. You can overcome life's obstacles if you have guts. When you have faith, you have a reason for trying.

It is a spiritual warfare without a doubt. Being able to trust God at all times is a must. Know that He has your best interests at heart. He will turn the fire up to test your faith . . . to see what you are made of. He's checking you out under pressure. Can you take it?

My struggles are over. I know I can make it. I'm determined to enjoy my life. I'm learning to appreciate the journey. Life isn't always going to be great. I'm not going to allow the bad days to overshadow the good ones. Expanding faith to higher dimensions is awesome for the soul. God is not to blame for our circumstances or our misfortunes. It is not God's fault that you are not where you feel you should be. Please stop saying "Lord, why have you allowed this to happen?" Stop pointing the finger at everyone else besides yourself.

Keep in mind that in order to get where you are going, you must take inventory where you are right now. This is not the finished product. This is the process, a phase that will truly pass. So straighten up your clothes. Take a moment to reclaim your faith. I dare you to attempt to extend your faith to a level that will surprise yourself. If you were to grade your faith, where would you stand? Faith is the engine which starts the vehicle. There is no substitute for faith. Give life to your faith. Let faith be the reason for never giving up.

I'm completely confident in God. I will continue to strive for spiritual improvement and take time to tune up my spirit. As you would feed your hungry cravings, so should you feed your spiritual appetite.

You will never know how strong your faith is until it's tested. Can your faith survive the challenges life presents? Storm after storm, Faith is a necessity would you not agree?

I believe with all my heart that God hears each and every single one of my dreams and goals and aspirations. He knows my fears as well as my goings and comings. It is He who created me, and He promised us that He would take care of us. He tests us severely. Yes, He does. But he said if I dare to wait for Him and trust in Him, it would not be in vain. I'm putting my heart and faith on the line.

I will be able to stand through the storms, through the dark rainy days and long nights. Faith does not go untested. Your faith will update you. It will let you know when it's time for its check up. Thank you, Almighty Great God for gracing me with faith after the doctors counted me out. The wind had been totally knocked out of me, as if I'd been hit by a speeding vehicle. Well, right there that is enough to say my faith has brought me through it all. It can only grow stronger. It can only be heightened. Whatever you believe, it can become your reality, if you have the faith.

There's nothing, nowhere, no one or no place that comes before God. I have come to know Him, but my faith continues to be tested. I made up my mind to utilize what God has given me so freely:

A Kept Promise

Life. There's so much waiting for all of us. Faith keeps me wide eyed and excited for what's to come. Faith is the sun in darkness. I can truly say my faith now has backbone.

It's such a soothing feeling knowing that God has my back. There are so many days I know I did not deserve it. He stood by me anyway. Many times I knew better and still went to the edge and jumped. Like always, He throws me a rope and pulls me through. We must be open towards the directions from God. If you listen to that voice within, it will never mislead you. I know when I ignore it, I always regret it.

Your Faith will never be in vain. You can tell how great your blessings by the size of your trials.

It does not matter how difficult, insurmountable, or overwhelming a situation becomes, there's always some good in it. God is more than capable of taking care of you. Don't become flustered when you feel God did not answer you when you thought He should have. It's never about us. It's His plan. There are reasons why He does what He does.

Both of my hands are thrown up in the air. I gave it all over to Him. Since I laid my burdens down, I tell you life has been much easier.

God is the constant all inclusive presence of good. He's a forceful, awesome, flawless wonder.

I love the spirit God has given to me. I love the fact that He continues to clear my path and make it clear for me to step toward my destiny. He has been my everything, and I need him to run this race. Don't abort your purpose. You will achieve all you believe.

God will never stop protecting or guiding us, twisting or turning us, or pulling and pushing us. He does whatever it takes to make sure our faith remains in tack. God watches with all delight when we discover our buried treasures. He has given each and every one of us hidden treasures. It's up to us to find them.

God has an unstoppable supply of goodness for all of us.

*****

Thought for the day:
Magnify God, not your problem.

A Kept Promise

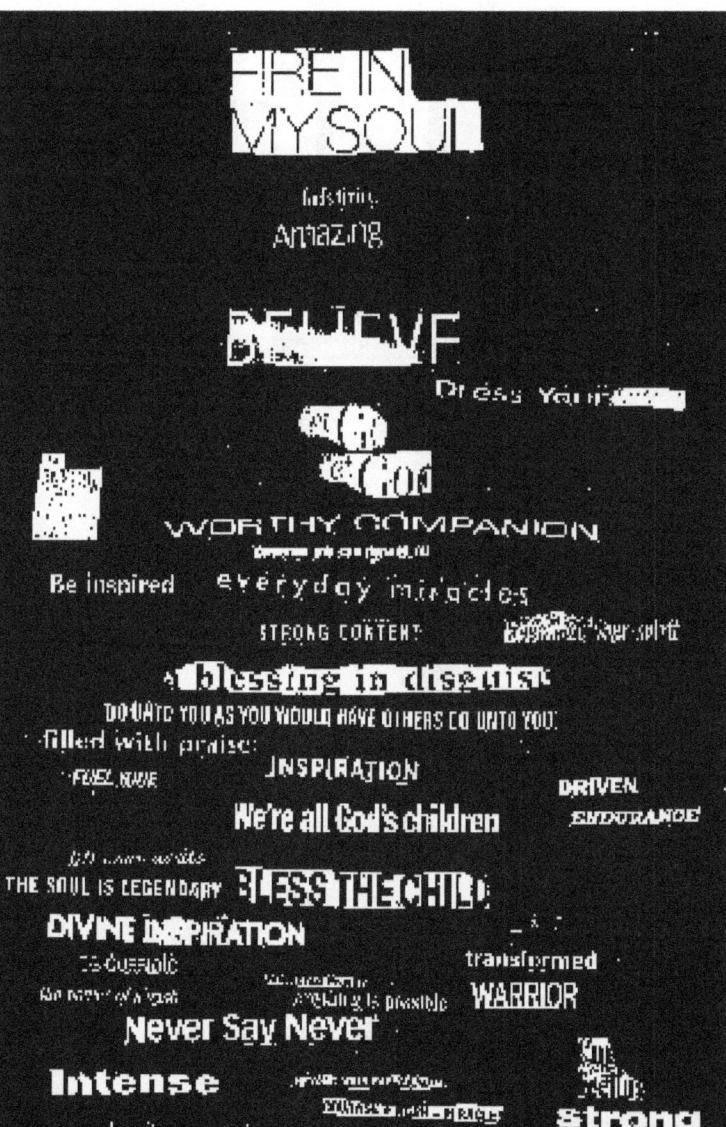

GO FOR IT

"Let us not grow weary while doing good. For in due season we shall reap if we do not lose heart."
Galatians 6:9

There's a certain energy that flows through the universe when you have your mind made up to

A Kept Promise

do something. Why do some of us have to go through high waters and low valleys before realizing enough is enough? When your mind is made up, really made up, there's no stopping you.

How badly do you want it? How far are you willing to reach?

When things seem impossible, are you willing to let it go? Whatever it is that you want, whatever it may be: a new job, a home, a new body, a new life. Whatever. Go for it. Go for it.

Write out your plan. Stick to it and start stepping. Step into the direction in which you are aiming. Don't concern yourself with things that distract you or things that hinder you. Like the bull in the arena kicking his feet in the dirt and his eyes. Fiercely focus on the red cloth. That's how you have to be when you want something.

You will never get it done thinking about it or wishing upon it. If you're happy living life on a normal basis, that's great. But if you're the one who likes to take it to higher grounds, then I'm talking to you. Step it up a notch. Give a little extra. Release that dream that's inside your soul. Give birth to it. Leaving your dreams to chance and having it on auto pilot doesn't get the job done.

Utilize your ability for higher sights. Try the impossible! By all means, don't get too comfortable. My friend, comfort can be a dangerous zone. If you're reaching for higher grounds, comfort will keep you from making a home run. It's easy to get stuck. On your mark, get set, are you ready? What are you waiting for? Go for that feeling that makes you skip a double beat. Grab life by the horns and enjoy the ride. Make it worth while.

I love keeping life fun. And if I sat around waiting for anyone to give me what I want, I'd be a sad puppy. I constantly keep my spirit entertained. I am my own marching band. There are times I've been the cheerleader as well. To me, life is all about doing what you truly honestly desire. It's what gets your heart pumping. Dare to go beyond your vision. Dare to make it happen.

Invest in the things that are going to make this journey for you a pleasant one. A happy one. Ride first class. (Why not?) The only limits we have are the ones we put on ourselves. What a total waste to leave this life and not dare go after any of your desires. Don't be afraid. Let go of fear and don't be afraid to fail. Truly speaking, you never fail as long as you try. Step in and through your fears, reach for the moon and if by chance you fall, you'll land among the stars. Reach, you are almost there. Don't let go.

It's not about your situation. It's about your destination. Don't get discouraged when things are at a standstill. This is when character is built. When reaching for higher grounds, grab hold and don't let go. Remind yourself constantly of your ambitions and goals. It doesn't matter how far down you have fallen into a pit. Know that it's not over. Tomorrow is a brand new day.

Keep your eyes on the prize! Go for it with heart and with gusto. Whatever area in your life that you have fallen short, don't be so hard on yourself. Get up and try again and again. Don't procrastinate. Procrastination is deadly. Don't look to the left or to the right. Look straight ahead and make it happen in this lifetime. One thing for sure is we do not get another chance at this life. So if there are things you want to achieve, I suggest you go that extra mile and give a little extra and reach a little higher. Push the envelope to the next level. Dare to step out of your comfort zone. Dare to keep the promise you made to yourself to take it all the way. Dare to stay committed to succeeding. Give birth to your visions. Make it happen. Dismiss all of your fears and all that's weighing you down.

Be you at all times, and let no one ever try to make you feel bad or less than you are for being you. Express yourself. If you can not live your dreams, then what's the point of being here? Find the direction you're heading and march on.

Always continue to raise the bar higher. You can't just accomplish one or two goals and be content. Keep it going. Don't stop until you have it all.

Who says you have to settle for less? Never settle for less than you're worth. You're better than for what you give yourself credit. You have it right in the palms of your hands. What are you going to do with it? Blaming others for why you are not where you should be is the biggest no-no! People only go as far as you allow them to go, and that's a fact! Take charge and control of your destiny. Have no regrets. There's no point. Whether you should or should not have, you can't bring back time. Complaining does not help. Not to mention people don't want to hear it. What's the point of going through life nagging, mopping and dragging? Put some pep in your step. Reinvent you.

You can't afford to wait. I said it to you once before: Federal Express is not arriving with your passions in its truck. If you really want something and you give up before achieving it, then you didn't want it as bad as you thought. Get it. Whatever it is you want. Go and get it.

What a waste to leave this earth and not play out every song in our hearts. Only you know what it is you truly desire. Run this race with your best shot. You can't expect your ship to come in if you haven't sent one out. It takes work to get to your goals and more work to maintain them. Nike says it best and very simple: *Just do it.* Straight to the point.

When your stress level is on overdrive and sanity is many miles away, get a grip . . . and fast. Don't let the madness drive you insane. Be grateful with what you have been given. Stick to your guns and know all will work out for the best. Everything is working for good. You can go after your dreams and you can have them. Get what you want out of life. You can have your cake and eat it too, along with the ice cream and the balloons (yes, but don't eat the balloons). At any age! Don't put restrictions on yourself. Be fierce and fabulous. Be inspired to always climb higher. Go beyond your own expectations. Travel down a new road. Wake up old dreams and create new ones. Capture a new gleam of hope.

The road in life has many changes, and when things don't go according to your plan, it is not the end of the world. Remember it's not over. All you do now is find a different route. Invent one if necessary. There's more than one way to get the job done.

When you tried your best and you didn't

A Kept Promise

succeed, get up and try again. Here's a verse from the Bible that totally inspires me: *"Therefore we also, since we are surrounded by so great a cloud of witness, let us lay aside every weight and the sin which so easily ensnares us and let us run with endurance the race that is set before us."* Hebrews 12:1-2.

That is so powerful. Run your race with all that inside of your being.

You are an important instrument in the symphony of life. Make sure you carry your own tune. Make a statement. When it's your turn to check out of this life, make sure you have left your mark. No one can be you, but you. There will only ever be one you. You're unique, exquisite, and special. If no one has told you, I'm telling you now. And you better know it.

I don't care what you've been through. I will repeat that. I don't care what you've been through. You can make it. Don't let anyone tell you otherwise.

Let me encourage you to hold on like you have never held on before. Can I encourage you to get back up? After the storm has left you, know that you will breathe again. Sooner or later all the pieces will fall in place.

I do not claim to know it all. Who does? I know one thing for a fact, though: the universe responds when you send out signals. Go and get what you want. You cannot wait for someone to hand it over to you. Only you know what it is that you want and what it will take to get it. You are the only one who can put limits on yourself.

Don't let anything or anyone hold you back from having a totally fulfilled life. Don't wait to become a certain size, age, or status change before you appreciate these precious moments. Make life exciting and entertaining. Follow impulse urges. Satisfy new desires. After all, this is your life.

Feed your cravings for life. Live out your full potentials. Dare to step towards the unknown. Be willing to take risks. Dance to the music you hear inside your soul. Grab on and trust the Almighty.

There's no reason at all you should not have what you want. You deserve to have each one of your desires fulfilled. How are you going to tell your story? As for me, I want to tell it well and not leave any stones unturned.

Never be intimidated. Walk like you know you know. Don't just think about what you want. Take action. Surely it will all come to fruition. Take your wings and soar like an eagle. Fly as high as you can fly. There comes a time when you know it's time to do what you must. You've taken enough madness. You've been settled, or maybe unsettled, for far too long. You pretty much have had it. There's only one way to go from this point and that's up and to do that is up to you. You know the time to upgrade your status is past due. Get the polish out and shine up those rough edges. Do not let your life pass you by and you're left with regrets. You deserve to have all the grand gifts life has to offer.

Step up and claim your prize despite of all your mistakes, disappointments, rough times and changing times. Get what you're seeking. Change is a very challenging experience. At times it can be painful. Change is necessary for growth. Don't become comfortable with discomfort. Seek your passion.

Go for the dream that keeps coming back . . . your destiny. Keep inspiring yourself to be you. Don't let the light burn out before you reach your destination. Keep stepping up to the plate. You have to be persistent about it.

Lack of commitment and loss of enthusiasm are quick ways for dreams to diminish. It can become difficult and discouraging when all your efforts seem in vain. Create ways to keep your dreams alive. It is absolutely essential that you do not give up. You must hold on to it until it has come to pass. The more difficult the trail, the more rewarding the prize. I have seen people talk themselves out of their dream. They begin focusing on all the obstacles and the work it takes to get the job done. Before you know it, another dream has gone into hiding. Dreams keep the soul alive. Don't just take notices of your dreams, take action. Fulfill each and every one of them. If you don't know where you're going, any road will take you there. Know where you're going.

Get out and go when you're down to nothing. God is up to something. Don't lose hope when your plans aren't going according to how you thought. Finishing is much better than starting. Anyone can start something. Are you capable of seeing it through?

Cheer others on as you would want to be cheered on. Your turn is next. Whatever it takes to conquer, it is the same antidote to keep it. I tell you. I look at how fast time is flying, and I realize a couple of things. One, it is not over yet. Two, there's no time. None! To not follow what's inside of my heart, what do I have to lose? Sanity? Those who know me know that is gone already.

Take risks, embrace the unknown. Accept the challenge from the universe to experience new endeavors. There's nothing stopping you but perhaps yourself. You have been given the opportunity to express your being. Do your dance and do it well. There's enough for everyone. No need to concern yourself with who has what.

What are your passionate desires? Are you living them? Or have you put them away? Have you allowed yourself to stop trying? Have the storms of life knocked you down one time too many? If you happen to be in this stage of your life where chaos has moved in, accept it. Embrace it. Learn and buckle up. You are going to make it. Never stop trying. If you wait for guarantees, you will miss the shebang. When you have that burning desire, act upon it.

Fear is such an issue with so many people who are so afraid of what may not happen. Never giving life to the "what ifs." What if: you tried a little harder? Pushed a little stronger? What if it all turns out right?

You have the power to choose how you live your life. It doesn't matter what cards you're dealt. It matters how you play them. Decisions have power. Make the right ones. Be confident with who you are and work it.

It's not what you dare; it's about what you dare to do. It's not what you drive, it's what drives you! Light way actions produce light way results. Chances never taken are a lifeless dream.

Every life has its own rhythm.

A Kept Promise

Stay excited about your desires. Don't look for anything or anyone to complete you. Don't stop now. You've started your quest for self and desires. Don't whither away to mediocrity. Please, no offense to those who are comfortable with mediocrity. Who can deny how endless the boundaries are?

If you encounter a dead end upon your journey, do not spend the energy on it. Find an alternative route and stop moping. Pain produces power. Your desires and passions must stay on fire. If things are not happening fast enough perhaps you should turn up the heat. Your ultimate dreams are obtainable.

Dismiss the restriction you have unconsciously welcomed. Some people are given mountains and climb them. Some people are given hills and never make it.

Do not leave this life wishing you could have done more.

There are no success stories without disappointments. There is no winning without failure. No light days without dark ones.

Keep rolling with the punches. Ride the waves like a boxer in an arena dodging and ducking the swings; you must remain standing and not allow life to knock you out.

Qualities that are essential for success include self motivation, determination, self esteem, enthusiasm, persistence, flexibility, thick skinned, positive attitude and direction.

Keep one thing in mind: wishing for something to happen is different from working towards making it happen.

The universe has no choice but to comply when you have strong desires. When you have courage and God on your side, you're more than ready to do what needs to be done.

A fighter never gives up. Be inspired by your prize. What a great reward when you receive the benefits from all your efforts and hard works.

Concentrate on each and every one of your goals. Habitually apply your energy and actions towards them. The prize is victory if you do not become weary! This race of life is not for the weak at heart.

It takes a winner, not a whiner, to tackle what life throws his way. Whiners sit and let life happen. Winners go out and make life happen. When planting your seeds, know that it will take time to go from the first declaration (the seed) to the final demonstration (the plant).

You deserve it! Go on and get yours. All of it!

Your life can be as stupendous, spontaneous, adventurous, and passionate as you want it to be. Allow life to live within you. Make a significant impact. Be forever young. Be forever you. Like a child lost in a toy store, have that same gleam of total bliss towards life.

I know that I am a totally full-grown woman. However, my heart and spirit will forever be young! May life give you enough happiness to make you sweet; enough trails to keep you strong; enough faith to keep you going. I wish upon you all a great fulfilled exciting life. Can I say that again? An exciting life!

*****

Thought for the day:
Who says the sky has to be the limit?

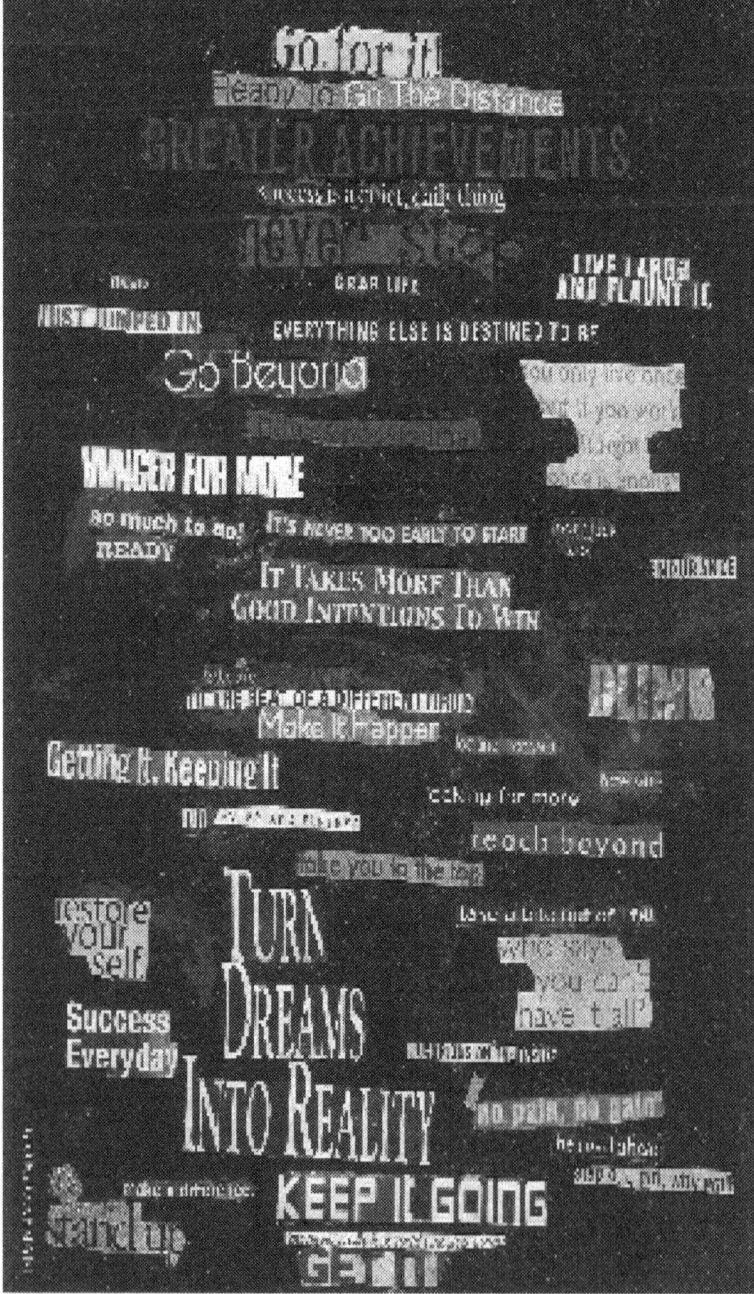

DRIVEN BY WAY OF GOD

It's something in my soul that just will not let me give up. Test after test! Battle after battle! Storm, tornado, earthquake, doctors counting me out . . . whatever crosses my path. I am totally determined to stay driven. I've come much too far to give up now.

I expected that each person I told that I was writing this book would be as thrilled about it as I was. It was a bit disappointing to realize that everyone isn't going to give you the same enthusiasm you give out, and that's fine. When you are driven, nothing will stand in your way. A champion is someone who gets up even when he can't. Keep life flowing and growing. You will never get to second base if your foot is still on first. Keep at it. You will hit a home run. Concentrate on your attributes and not character faults. I say that a lot.

So if you've fallen off track, take a deep breath, count to ten or maybe to twenty, and try it again. Sometimes you need more than plan B. You need C, D, E, F and G. Can I get a witness? I've been taught a winner never quits and a quitter never wins.

Everyone has drive. You have to feed that drive and nourish it. Some people give up too fast.

They tried a few times they gave eighty percent, perhaps even one hundred, and things didn't work out the way it was planned. And there it goes back on the back burner, and every once in a while the drive gets heated up. Within no time, it gets cold. You've got to want it bad enough. For twenty years I wanted to write this book. The more I thought about it, the more I wanted it. I'd write a couple of pages and get caught up in nothing and back to my mind the book went. One day I decided this is it. I wanted to do it bad enough and I did it. There is nothing to it but to do it. That is a fact. Actions always spoke louder than words.

There will be days when if feels like all your get up and go has got up and left, and the more you give the less you receive, and the sun is nowhere in sight. I know someone knows what I mean. Don't get bitter, get better.

Go somewhere to recharge your battery, and like a Timex watch, you must take a licking and keep on ticking.

Stay hungry for life. Stay close to people who make things happen. Keep your drive ignited. Keep it burning. It does not matter how many times you fail at something. I don't care how many times you become disappointed. You can't let anyone keep you from reaching your dreams.

I know it all sounds good. Easier said than done. Truth of the matter it is all up to you. If you are fifty years old and you want to go back to school, it's all about you.

Conquer your fears. Look within yourself and find out what it is that drives you. What is it that gets your motor running? What is it that turns

A Kept Promise

on your lights? What is it that puts your mind in the euphoric state? Doesn't matter how outrageous or insane it sounds to anyone, if it rocks your boat, then you better work. Learn to entertain your spirit and accommodate your soul. Become your own best friend. Sometimes you have to be your own fan club.

I'm driven by the spirit of the Almighty. It's the most awesome feeling when you feel that deep spiritual connection. When you are in tune with the universe, what a feeling!

The true test comes when your sanity is being tested. Everything around you has gone past chaotic, and you still maintain your composure. Now that's when you know you have arrived in the sanity zone of life.

We are not on this Earth forever. This is it. So what time do you have to spend on things that really do not matter? Where's that time? It doesn't exist. Step toward you. Bring out what is inside of you. Bring it out. Keep the oomph in your life. Keep it interesting. One of my many favorite quotes by Tony Robbins: *In order to get things you never had, you must do something you've never done.*

People respect winners. Winners always rise to the occasion. Be the winner that you are. Don't let all the things that went wrong in your life dampen your spirit or cause you to give up. Use your stumbling blocks as stepping stones. There will be times you may have to take a step back in order to take two and three steps up. Keep getting back up.

When a strong desire gets put on hold, it can hinder your spirit. I became serious and with the help of a friend pushing and encouraging me. That's why it's so vitally important to stay around positive people. They encourage and that is so important and so vital.

I wrote at every opportunity I had. I did in two months what I didn't do in twenty-three years. I had to light my drive on fire. I can not even begin to explain the feeling I had when I received the first draft of this book. Oh my God what a feeling! When your drive comes to life—now we're talking.

When that fire is burning, don't stop until you extinguish it. Drive is what gives you the reason to rise.

The fire in my soul ignites when I look around at all the many blessings God has bestowed upon me. He's given me the best family, awesome true friends, and an attitude toward life that is truly a gift. Non-stop energy that is constantly flowing. I'm completely in awe of His wonders. I am driven by way of God and love every bit of it. I yearn for His instructions.

There are times when I become frustrated and discouraged at the obstacles and trials that come my way. Then I remind myself that this is part of the plan. God is not going to give me more than I can bear. There's a reason for everything. I've chosen to believe that. God knows all the secrets of the heart. I have had moments when I asked God for His help, and then I found myself trying to work it out. No longer. I completely and totally admit that I cannot do it. I tried. I have to give it all completely over to Him. I am no longer driving myself overboard over things that are out of my control.

I don't know about anyone else, but I know

that I could not run this race without God's mercy and grace. I say yes to God. I say yes to life. I say yes to me.

When you pray, you're talking to God. When you meditate, you are listening to Him. Take time to listen to what God has to say to you. Try His way. When I was about sixteen years old, I was in my room listening to my gospel music. I had my own phone line, and my friends would call and I would turn the music down. My mom caught me once and she asked if I was ashamed for my friends to hear that I was listening to gospel music. Before I could respond, she said that if you are ashamed of God on Earth, He'll be ashamed of you in Heaven.

Honor the giver of gifts. Never get to the point where you have attained large amounts of valuables and you lose touch with who made it all possible. You didn't think it was all about you, did you? Let His spirit guide you. Listen to that still voice that constantly speaks to you.

I've always felt God has a special watch over me. He birthed within my soul a great gift of life and what good is a gift if it can't be shared?

*****

Thought for the day:
Seek the giver and you will receive the gifts.

WHAT GOES AROUND COMES AROUND

When you give, give from the heart and because you want to give it. A giving spirit without expectation is a beautiful one. Whatever you give out comes back tenfold, whether it is spiritual or mental. How you give it will set the path on how it will return.

You cannot expect peace, love, prosperity and happiness if all you give is attitude, complications, and drama. Give out what you want. If you are looking for success, higher standards, and a clearer point of view and you do not receive them, perhaps you need to work on what you are issuing out.

Life is a boomerang. Be cautious on how you "throw it out." How you send it is how it will come back.

I want the very best in everything. I want a peaceful smooth cruise through this life. I give out what I want in return. With each person I meet, I share the gift of the Spirit . . . the gift of feeling absolutely divine to the fullest degree at all times. When you give out confidence, self esteem, and positive energy, how can anything else reside? You want success? You must look successful. You will attract who you really are. Be the kind of friend you want in return.

If you want inspiration, give inspiration.

Don't go around putting people down and then expect someone to cheer you on. It's great if you have it going on. You may have everything that you set out to achieve, and that is an awesome accomplishment. But there's nothing you can achieve that should make you feel you are above others. Humble yourself, if you haven't already.

You really don't want someone to snub you. Be aware whose face you are sticking your nose up to. One never knows what tomorrow will bring. If someone licks the red off your lollipop, no need to get out the revenge kit. Living well is the best revenge.

It's a relief to know that no matter what, everything will fall right into its place. That's why it's important to put out good. Serve it out the way you want it and it all will welcome you with open arms and a smile.

I want a lot in life. I don't mind putting out the work to receive the rewards. My challenge is when it becomes difficult and things are not working out as I think it should, I'm quick to put it all on pause. I've learned that's the time to tighten my grip, to dig my heals in the dirt and roll with the punches. Whoever said "no guts, no glory" . . . did he ever know what he was talking about! Rome wasn't built just on one's thoughts. It took action on a constant basis.

Appreciation is a kind of gesture. It's an enchanting feeling when you know you are appreciated. It's uplifting when everything you gave out didn't go unnoticed. When things don't go exactly according to your plans, there's no need to change your mind set. Give out the confirmation that all is well regardless of the matter.

Every action and thought is a signal to the universe to respond. Love is a wonderful seed to plant. Be extremely aware of your thoughts and attitudes towards others. Surely as the sun is to rise, karma is no surprise.

Be kind to one another. How dare any of us snub one another? Just thinking that we are higher or better shows a lack of humanity.

What web are you weaving around yourself? If you can't take it, then you should not dish it.

I recall a time when an ex-boyfriend of mine was a bit intoxicated. He was playing around. He fell and he fell hard. I laughed my guts out. My stomach was in cramps from laughing. Within twenty-four hours, we were walking out of a café and it was snowing. The ground was slippery. I went to grab his hand and missed. After recovering from the embarrassing moment, I discovered that my two front teeth were chipped. I no longer laugh at anyone!

Be the kind of friend you want to have. Keep in thought that every action has a reaction. For every stone one throws, two will be thrown back. So if you are throwing love, that's all that can return.

Sometimes something as small as a smile can brighten someone's day. Something so effortless can mean so much. In the midst of your very important busy hectic day, take time and share kindness. It's free and it really does go a long way.

Extend yourself to touch the soul of a man. Go on and go out of your way. You are given so you can give.

Say what you mean and mean what you say.

Nothing bugs me more than someone talking just to talk. Let me be more precise: the ones who say what they're going to do and how they're going to do it and it never comes about. I mean, what's the point of wasting all that air? I call them air talkers.

Be about your word. A word means a lot. If you say you are going to do something, then by all means stick to it.

God is the one true force that has remained constant and true. People are constantly changing. The ones you thought were genuine and authentic are the ones who pierce your heart the deepest. The ones you didn't give a second may have surprised you with such unexpected joy. Constant cautions of your actions will never lead you astray.

CARRY ON

Can you carry on when your heart is breaking? When the fire in your dreams has completely burned out? Can you carry on?

In life you have to have a strong will, a brave heart and a courageous spirit.

Whatever you go through, whoever left you or whoever you lost . . . or just to maintain sanity, you must always carry on. Trials come to make you stronger. When the trials become more challenging and your reserve nerves have had it, breathe, smile and recharge. Recharge the necessary tools that fuel your spirit. Discharge all things that weigh you down.

With lack of persistence, your chances of failing become possible. Having the ability to press forward when you have been knocked down, shows signs of a winner and winners always win.

If you are not in it for the long haul, why start? Finish the things you begin. If you don't, how will you ever know the outcome? Whether you win or lose, you saw it through. And see it through you must do. Don't get disappointed at disappointment. People will let you down time and time again. Learn who to deal with. You know the saying, "Fool me once, shame on you. Fool me twice, shame on me." Don't get distracted when distraction comes around.

That door will open. Keep knocking. Continue to pursue all you believe you can. I've seen so many people start off passionately. They gave it all in the beginning, then fizzled out for various reasons like love, drugs, or lack of enthusiasm. What a waste to give up on one's dreams. Keep surviving towards the madness. You're bound to end up just where you want.

When life lays obstacles in front of you and that mountains are higher than you thought, go ahead and rest for a moment. Then you must get back up and tackle the task at hand. Your dreams will blossom when it's your time. You know you have what it takes. There are dreams right now stirring within your soul. Have heart enough to embrace them. Run your race to its full course. I must admit, that when love came my way, I put everything on hold. Pathetic, I know.

To put my dreams on pause while I entertained what I thought was love, again was pathetic. I know now that true love allows you to be you. It encourages you. It supports you. I've learned the hard way. If it doesn't fit, do not force it. If it doesn't go with the flow, let it go. Long story, don't let people or things keep you from you. After the end of the day, what is it that you want? Life's journey is great! It's the detours that are the concerns.

If Hell has broken out and you're going through the fire and the pressure is building everywhere, you know what to do? Right? Yes! You said it. Carry on!

Martha Wash from the Weather Girls has a song called *Carry On*. A line from that song which I love says "when the valley was deep, I stood strong. I carried on." Truly speaking, that's all you can do.

What sense does it make to stop in the middle of the stream?

When my faith was being tested with my health, and the clouds were becoming darker by the hour, I knew I was not going to throw in the towel. No way! I had to lift myself up and dig deep to pull out the survival kit. One step at a time my soul forced me to keep stepping. You can't look to the left or the right. You must look forward and forward only.

One wrong turn can send you in a completely different direction. I do mean completely. One evening while setting out to visit one of my cousins in the hospital, my Mom and I were twenty minutes away, and with one wrong turn we ended up miles away. Frustration was at its peak. Finally when heading in the right direction, an hour and a half later, traffic backed up and we were at a standstill. Right then and there, who calls? Mother Nature. I had two full glasses of water. My knees were rocking and rolling. My dear God, send sanity immediately. Finally, we arrived. I felt as if I had walked from China to London. One wrong turn, just one, can send you in a completely different direction. Don't let a wrong turn keep you from the direction you are heading. Endure and stay focused to get your mission accomplished.

When you're having one of those days and you are in a bad mood and everyone needs to get out of your way and you're so mad you have smoke coming out of your nostrils and you are like a time bomb that's seconds away from going off, take a deep breath and redirect that energy. Overloading is not healthy.

The race isn't won by the one who completes the race first. It is won by the survivor who was able to go forth and who can continue through all the disappointments and trials. That is who the award goes to. Do not allow yourself options to give up. Carry it out to the finish.

Stay focused. Keep your target in sight.

While working on this book day and night for months, I was blown to bits when transferring it to a disc, seeing all my writing compacted. It was at that moment I realized I was not halfway to being finished. And I thought I was almost done.

I was unaware of the task at hand. But to finish it was what I wanted. Frustration can cause dreams to be denied. I could not allow that. I had to look on the bright side. At least, I had started. One has to be able to carry it through. Starting is good. Completing a goal is excellent.

I had to finish. I'm good at telling others how to do it. How could I encourage others and not be a example myself?

Move over Dorothy; make room for me on the "Yellow brick Road."

Here's another fact: Thinking about things does not get the job done!

You must have the tools of your trade. If your plans are to fly like the eagles, you have to stop chatting with the ducks. It's okay to smile, but when you have a destination that you are trying to reach, you must surround yourself with the surrounding associated with your destination.

When I couldn't go any further, God carried me. When I couldn't take it any more, He stepped in and took control. I always knew that I had a lot to give. We are so much stronger than we credit ourselves to be. Life will definitely force you to see what you are made of. It will give you a run for your sanity. I know I have a witness somewhere! The strong are the only ones that survive. I know I can not afford to quit. I can afford to give up on hope. I refuse to throw in the towel. I'm going to be that older woman in my eighties skating at the beach at six a.m. Some think that because one grows older, one looses the enthusiasm for life? Nonsense! As long as you have breath in your being, it's not over. Once you close your eyes—that's the finale! So dance it out fiercely. Keep striving! Your blessings are soon arriving.

If you're in the stage of your life where you feel enough is enough, each tornado is more severe than the last, and your breaking point is within reach, I encourage you to find something strong and concrete to hold on to. Emerge with the right ammunition to support your journey and keep on keeping on.

Carry your own weight, my dad used to say when we were kids. Get your own. *Stand up and never ask anyone for anything* are words I'm delighted to replay in my thoughts. With my mom constantly pushing faith and my Dad having a "can-do" attitude, I found the mixture to be quite rewarding for me. Nothing can keep me from me. I will run this race with every bit of finesse I can muster.

I'm not going anywhere! I'm in it to win it. There have been times where just for a half a second, the thought of quitting tried to creep into my thoughts. Then it was quickly replaced by the strong intense will to succeed.

A Kept Promise

Make a promise to yourself to forge onward regardless of the results.

*****

Looking from within
This time I must win
Giving life my best
Who has time for regrets?
Finger pointing gets you nowhere
The nonsense I can no longer bare
Stepping up to the plate
What time is there to hesitate?

UNDER CONSTRUCTION

Oh my God! The transformation from caterpillar to butterfly is not the smoothest transition, but a very rewarding one. After all the mistakes repeatedly made and all the jumping in the pool when you knew there was no water there, but jumped anyway . . . and had the nerve to complain your head was bumped. Could I be talking from experience? But of course. The things we go through before we get it. I am appalled at all of the unnecessary aggravations I have caused myself. I look back and can't help but laugh. Why didn't I listen to what my parents told me to avoid? The best lesson is a well earned one.

The many things I searched for and sought out was at the very place I started from. ME!!!

There are a few minor repairs that must be done. After all, even a brand new car goes in for a tune-up. While under construction, tenaciously work on yourself. Saturate your soul with enthusiasm. Commit yourself to something other than insanity. Stay true to you. Do something you haven't done in a while and take care of you.

I believe in defining gravity. Keep yourself together. Just because one gets older doesn't mean it all goes downhill. I think of myself like wine. It only gets better with time. You are a cut above so have a first class attitude on how you see yourself. You're not being cocky. It's confidence. You may not presently be where you know you are on your way to and that's okay. Love yourself through the process. Just as night will turn to day, it's going to all go your way! Continue to build and learn and don't forget to enjoy the construction. Be yourself and love every single second of it.

There's so much more to you and you know it. Take off the mask and reveal who you really are. You are one of a kind. There is something so special that only you possess. Own it! Love it! Treasure it! Welcome all facets of yourself.

I've learned that you can never be too careful. The best way to solve a problem is to avoid it. What I mean about that is that there are some headaches that we can avoid! Anything that tears you down rather than help build you up must not become part of your "must haves." While going through the changing hands of time and the unexpected turns, strong will and heart are great tools to have handy. What area in your life needs a face lift, a little upkeep, or a maintenance upgrade?

Try not to become undone or unraveled through the course of your trial. Get yourself a tube of super glue and keep it handy to keep the pieces together. (Teasing about the glue . . . if you need glue to keep yourself together, you need more help than *any* book can give you.) When the storms start raging, who wants to go through the dark stages of your life without light? Know that broken pieces can be mended.

I admit I like looking much younger than my age. I like looking fit. It takes effort. It takes more than wishing for it. It would be nice to eat any and every thing and have the body of a twenty-year old. I mean who wouldn't want that? Fitness is important. It's connected to a more fulfilled life. It's not about the size. It's about your health.

If you have mistreated yourself in the past, go and get yourself a repair kit. Patch up the necessary fixtures. You have no excuses as to why you cannot improve your health status. We make a million and one excuses why we can not work out, or we complain that eating healthy is too expensive. Always take time out for yourself. You're never too young or too old to get healthy. I recall when I was younger, I could dab a little cream here and there and be good to go. Now it's triple action extra strength multi-task products!

You do what has to be done.

As a child, my parents constantly instilled in my siblings and me to never give up, and for us to pursue our desires with strong passions. Growing up, I had so many dreams I had to decide which direction to go in first. At times it became overwhelming just by the thoughts alone. Trying to be a jack of all trades, one winds up being a master at none. So today is all about taking one desire at a time. It's about conquering all the fears and maintaining the ability to stay sane while going through the transformation of being beautifully sculptured. Stand strong and firm. Sweat not the small stuff as there's no time for that. Every life has its own rhythm.

Revolving in our true existence is what we all strive for. We are all looking for that space in our lives where all is perfect. Smooth sailing and no interruptions are thoughts from a fairy-tale land. In the real world, things aren't that simple. Can you stay uncorrupted and untainted through the construction of your transformation process? Life is going to be life and life will run its course.

Maintaining composure when the heat has risen takes a strong character. I'm the first to admit that when things don't go my way or the way I expected it to go, I can go from one hundred ninety to three below zero in the matter of seconds.

I'm learning to redirect that energy and turn it into more productive venues. I know through the difficulties I will come out a better person. There has to be a reason why we go through what we go through. What doesn't kill us makes us stronger. How many times have we heard that one? Truth of the matter is that is a true statement. One does not get through this life without some form of challenge. Life will force us to see who we are.

It starts from the making over the inside. That's where the true essence of beauty begins. Some areas you possess may be flawless to the bone. It's the department that is in need of repairing that you should address and do the necessary adjusting. Reacquaint yourself with your blueprints.

When you build with the wrong tools, don't be surprised when it falls through. Doing it right the first time avoids a returned trip. We grow through the turning wheel of life. Through all the turns you will learn. From each change and twist you will learn. Your building may be the last to be developed, but you are increasing the value. More value requires more work. Throughout every level of your quest you will learn. Be grateful for the experience.

My moments for searching for my soul and searching for that sacred place we all reach for has been a bit challenging at times to say the least. The constant change of coming into your own sometimes can get you close to the edge.

Do not get used to the same routine. For God's sake, add a touch of salsa! The thing that tried to break you down, turn it around and let it become what builds you. Keep in mind there aren't any mistakes, only lessons. Some are more costly than others.

When arrows start flying each and every which way and you're as low as you could go, it's time to venture towards a new direction.

Don't resist change. Flexibility is necessary. It's the common factor for the success. When the pressure is on, it is time to remember transition isn't always pleasant.

I know that at certain stages during my journey, had I known what was arriving, I would have pressed the fast forward button. It is now obvious that it all had to happen the way it did. Those roads lead me to an exciting one.

Be able to deal with any situation when presented. Your transition is your molding process. A diamond doesn't shine with a snap of a finger. A diamond is cut again and again until it is at its best.

The drive for spiritual improvement is a constant desire for me. If my spirit is right, I'm good to go. Thank God I've learned to channel all my emotions in their proper direction. You will learn how strong you are during your darkest moments. The discovery of is awesome.

I'm ok with all the mistakes I've made. I can't do anything but learn, right? I quit judging myself and others. Self discovery is an ongoing process. Enjoy your total being through all the stages. At times when you feel disconnected, know that it's temporary. Things you're unhappy with you can change. You'll never change what you tolerate.

I'm learning lessons on a daily basis. I'm learning to love me with all my short comings, flaws, and attributes plus or minus—you name it, honey! Like it or love it, all you can do is give your best.

I love that nostalgic feeling. I can be anything I want to be and being everything is what I want.

Today I realize I have all that I need. I'm in the prime of my life and all is perfectly well. (It really is.) All I ever wanted was to experience the greatest gifts life has to offer. I've traveled down unnecessary roads and gone to the edge a time or two. Heck, I've even jumped.

I've always managed to find my way back. I'm totally happy with who I am.

My best friend has a saying that I love: "Just because you step in manure, doesn't mean you have to smell like it." You could have walked through battery acid, hand wrestled a bear, and took a trip to hell and back, but the hard knocks don't have to be displayed.

BE GOOD TO YOURSELF

"Do everything in love." I Corinthians 16:14

If I've said it once, I've said it a thousand times: you are the best investment you can invest in. You are all you have. Why not take excellent superb top care of yourself? You deserve all you desire and then some. When those times come about and you don't make the smartest choices, don't beat yourself with a whip, do it with a feather. You are your worst critic. Give yourself a break.

Let your soul speak of the passions you exude. Do your heart some good and love it well. You are such an exquisite piece of art. Take a "me" day as often as possible. A "me" day is a day when it's all about you. It's a day when you cater to yourself and treat yourself to some extraordinary care. You are so overdue for that extra attention. I take a lot of "me" days. I treat myself well with every chance I get. Why not? Why shouldn't we reach for the highest star? God never said settling was mandatory. He said be grateful, and that is truly what I am.

There's so much more to life. So much more! Allow yourself to love yourself.

Cultivate the habit of treating yourself. Don't only pull out your finest china when you are entertaining guests. Cook a special dinner on your finest and play your favorite music and light the best smelling candles as you entertain you.

I recall one night my family had stopped by, and the ambience was so intriguing that they started looking for guests. They could not believe I had it completely laid out just for me.

Pampering is not a bad thing to have on your list. You present the image you project of yourself. If you don't care for yourself, without a doubt it will show.

The nicer you are to yourself, the nicer others will be to you. You cannot be good to anyone unless first you are good to yourself. Take time out for you. You must be your biggest support team. Take yourself out. Make a date with yourself. Treat yourself like royalty. Take time and find out who you are.

A lot of times people will give the reason for poor upkeep due to lack of funds. You do not have to make six figures to look like it. Hon, a box of baking soda does wonders.

A box of baking soda:

—mix with a tad of water and a few lemon drops until pasty. It makes the best face mask.

—twice a week is great for your teeth.

—while soaking in a hot bath, mix with your water.

—mix with oatmeal and a few drops of water makes a great face scrub.

The list is endless on ways to look like a million until you can collect it.

Be good to your phenomenal self and do it your way. Let your essences be known. I would never suggest anyone dimming their light because someone else chooses to leave his light off. When you give to yourself, it is such a pleasant experience.

You are an exuberant spirit. Life is here for the taking. Love yourself enough to surround yourself around people who feel the same way you do about yourself.

I never could fathom the thought of how people could want to kill themselves or harm themselves because someone does not love them. Please! Where's the love they should have for themselves? I know love can take a hold on you, but never should it take you away from yourself. To care more about someone else's opinion than yourself is not a healthy situation.

If by chance love takes you away from yourself, return quickly! Don't get me wrong and don't misunderstand me, loving someone is an absolutely beautiful experience. We all deserve it. I'm just no longer willing to lose myself to gain anyone!!

I am willing to compromise. I love myself enough now to care about how I feel and to care about what I want.

When a love affair goes haywire or someone isn't behaving the way you think they should, it could be plain and simple: They just don't love you. If so, it isn't the end. You should thank your lucky stars. They didn't deserve you anyway. You so deserve better. There's life after heart break.

When you really love yourself, there isn't time for short changing.

Whether you're young or young at heart, taking number one care of yourself should be your number one priority. There's nothing too good for you.

Constant pampering is not a crime. If it was, I would get life. Yes! I admit I love valet treatment. I'm not expecting anyone to give it to me. I gladly spoil myself. There are times I go overboard. Knowing that I pass this way once, I treat myself every chance I can. Who says you can't have cheese on your burger?

Traveling is one thing I consume myself with to keep my life interesting. One of my highlights on the journey was my move to Europe. To go to a foreign country and know not a soul and do quite well are treasured memories for me. Yes it's safe to say I am pretty good to myself.

*****

Thought for the day:
People see you as you see yourself.

GET OVER IT

Operation: Next! Alright! Already!

Moving right along. This is for the ones who can't get past all the wrongs and mistakes in their lives. It's not that serious. Do not focus on your defeats. Keep pressing forward. We all go through something.

When you find yourself in a situation that you could have avoided and it's no one's fault but yours, and your back really seems to be against the wall, remember the sweetest words of "This too shall pass." You got yourself into it and you will get yourself out of it.

You are a champion. You've known that from day one. You've made it this far and you know you will continue to make it!

You can come out of anything that has come upon you. You have the power inside of you to do so! Look at what's right and not wrong. You will be compensated for all of your troubles. When you get to that boiling point in your life, find somewhere or do something to let out the steam.

Don't bottle it in. You can't afford to fade into the woodwork. You have too much unfinished business to attend to. Get out of your rut, problem or issue. Speak *to* it and not about it.

No time for self pity. There's no time to wobble in "what ifs" and bad choices. Complaining doesn't solve anything. Do not use your mind or spirit for storage to store up yesterday's issues. Shake it off. It's too much trouble carrying around bitterness. Two tears in the bucket and . . . let it go!

I find myself at times banging my head against the wall (not literally of course) over issues that are totally out of my hands. Especially when people take your kindness for weakness—that bugs me the most. When you extend your hand to someone and they hit you with it. I will take advice from myself and get over it.

I know how frustrating it is when you put your trust in people and they turn out to be nothing at all as you expected. Our trust does not belong in man. Be glad when people show their true colors. It's best that they weave themselves out of your life.

Harping repeatedly over the same thing doesn't change the situation. I do believe venting is necessary. Once! When you start sounding like someone pressed your repeat button, you have crossed the edge. Move on to the next thing. Life is too short not to.

God will more than make up for all that has been taken from you. There's no time to play the blame game. Move up and on!

We can not afford to fret over losing materialistic or financial goods, for they all are temporary fixtures. If we lose our minds and soul, *then* it's time to fret. Who can afford to do that? It's not what you lose, it's what you gain.

There are no excuses for life ever getting the best of you. There's never a good enough reason to throw in the towel.

We've all been burned, whether by a friend or a relative. Each of us has encountered some form of disappointment. The choice is ours. If we stay focused on who wronged us, we will miss the true gift that is in store for us.

We are not here to take up space. We all have a mission to attend to. Sitting around whining about anything slows down progress. You need to dry your tears and throw your cares to the wind and start the stepping.

We are not here to take up space. If you have a mission to which to attend, such as heartbreaks, addictions or bad choices, move past it. Life is waiting for you. You will miss out if you don't learn how to what? Yes! Get Over It!

EPILOGUE

I hope that I have inspired you to take full advantage of every second of your privileged existence on this journey.
Remember to detoxify yourself from any and all insanity. There's no time or need to consume your precious life with unnecessary issues.
I don't know it all! One thing I know for a fact is: Life is as good as you make it. What you give to life, life will reciprocate it back to you.
What ever cards life has dealt you, play them to the best of your ability.
You owe no one an explanation for any of your expressions. You have been given the right to be yourself. Don't give that right away.
You have a light. It's up to you to turn it on. So, go pack up and ship off all your excess baggage and heavy loads. Flap your wings and fly. Put actions behind your passions.
We shall talk soon,

Debra Barre'

www.ingramcontent.com/pod-product-compliance
Lightning Source LLC
Chambersburg PA
CBHW020015050426
42450CB00005B/486